Come To Me and Drink

poems by

Julie Brooks Barbour

Finishing Line Press

Georgetown, Kentucky

Come To Me and Drink

ACKNOWLEDGMENTS

Many thanks to the editors of the publications in which the following poems appeared in various forms:

"Come To Me and Drink" and "Laundry Day," *inscape*
"Music for the Night, Music for the Day," *Kestrel*
"Starlings," *Sugar Mule*
"The Baby Discovers," *Taproot Literary Review*
"The First Step," *New Zoo Poetry Review*
"Watching," *roger*

I am grateful to the Kentucky Foundation for Women for an Artist Enrichment Grant in support of this work.

Editor: Christen Kincaid

Cover Art: Amelia Grace Brooks

Author Photo: Jude McConkey

Printed in the USA on acid-free paper.
Order online: www.finishinglinepress.com
also available on amazon.com

Author inquiries and mail orders:
Finishing Line Press
P. O. Box 1626
Georgetown, Kentucky 40324
U. S. A.

TABLE OF CONTENTS

for Eleanor Grace

Laundry Day

Corner by corner I hang the sheets:
dark blue, red, a floral print tattered at the edges.
They whip themselves into one another
with the breeze, sometimes twisting

into a snarl. My mother would drape her white sheets
one over two lines, a tent I would run through.
I show my daughter what I used to do.

She follows with mud under her fingernails,
hair hanging in her face, her smile the same
as any child dirty among the wash.

Next door my neighbor's white shirts
flap like sails, armpits stained yellow.
Across the street the widow hangs her briefs to dry.
It is a bright, clear day among the houses.

Dust To Dust

True natives,
we eat with dust in our mouths,

grit in our teeth.
Some days dust hides the world from me,

my children from me.
I fish with wet cloths for their mouths,

fighting the choking dirt
that lines the creases of my palms

and the seams of my dress,
dusts my brown hair black,

settles between my sheets,
swirls and curls over the floor.

It's a wonder we live.
But if one of us were to give in,

lay down for final rest on this soil,
it would never take us in.

It's too worn to hold even itself.
Like powder, it takes to the wind.

Cleaning
for Angela Vogel

Never mind the mess? I say not.
Check the aisles: miles and miles

of supplies to aid this chore,
myriad colors and scents

to make it more pleasant,
spots on the telly

of every woman giddy. Why,
this job can be done with such ease!

Yet I wait, procrastinate,
blame my lax on Mother

who also hates disorder.
Over the wire we complain,

consider rising up
then sit down.

I survey the damage:
a stray sock on the floor,

a crumpled gum wrapper,
dishes piling up, spilling over,

toys scattered.
I sigh, say goodbye,

and slowly rise
to the challenge of every day.

Bedrest

The world puts itself on hold, weighing trees
and power lines with ice, quieting electric hums.
The apartment grows colder, the furnace stopped.
Child, hold on. This city is no home for you yet.
The cats burrow under blankets and the dog
seeks humans for heat, but curtains hung in a doorway
will not keep you warm. Stars in the black sky,
once muted by streetlights, do not offer beams
bright enough to see by. I try to imitate the stillness
of the world outside, but a bitter bed is no safe haven.
Hold on, child, hold on.

Blood

What looks like blood from my mouth,
perhaps a tiny spattering from an irritated gum,
is only the apple's inner fruit turning brown
when exposed to air. Both dark, letting into the earth.
As essential as air and water yet not an element,
not fire, but life, juice of the grapes raised
in its place as a sacrament. It is not a peacemaker
or mercenary. It makes its home at opposite poles:
the beginning of violence and the beginning of hope,
one man dead and the other saved.
At either end, someone sends out prayers.

Panic Wheel

They wave from the top of the wheel,
my husband and daughter,
their seat rocking while a pair of passengers depart.
They lean precariously
over the seat's edge to see me, small from there,
then laugh as the ride begins,
the girl kicking her legs to become a blur.

I root my feet to the soil.
From the ground the wheel looks
as if it might come unhinged like a metal toy
and with its momentum
spin over the mountains,
the drop ringing thunderous from its weight,

seats crashing into rock,
metal bars strewn across trees,
photos in the morning paper.
Still it spins, secure.
Still my daughter squeals with glee
while my roots grow deep,
holding me fast to the earth.

Watching

It was a haunting, a shadow:
a hawk making a meal of crow
on my patio. I watched
the hawk pick his prey clean,
gulping strips of flesh.
Then he vanished.
I craned my neck to see what was left:
a skeleton, perfectly intact—
a museum piece—
reflecting the late-afternoon light.
On the other side of the patio,
my young daughter stood at the door,
palms pressed against the glass.
Neither she nor I stirred.
It was a moment left to itself,
a vision I woke from in the morning
and kept glancing back toward
with a mother's attentive eye
that could only watch.

Starlings

While I rock my daughter to sleep,
fledglings try their wings
on the other side of the window,

flapping up and down so crookedly
it's as if they were on strings.
The phone rings. The timer dings.

The old desires rise up:
dancing, laughter, familiar faces from my youth.
I rock them to sleep with the baby,

back and forth, ignoring the phone,
the supper in the oven.
Let it all burn.

The young birds outside are learning
to light on tree branches and shoot toward
the clouds. The baby sighs and shifts

into slumber. I put myself at ease
admiring the birds' black feathers
as the sun shimmers them green.

Leaving

The back door snaps into its frame,
a lid closing on a box.
Its pane reflects the rising sun
and my face searching for my infant
asleep in the bassinet
on the other side of the glass.
My black heels scatter pebbles
from the patio into the noiseless grass.
I step lightly, cautiously,
toward the driveway,
toward the world.
My hand lifts the car door's handle
and the heavy door inches open.
One high heel, then another.
My face reflected in the rearview mirror:
lipstick, hairstyle—
some other woman.
The motor whirrs to life.

Because the days are not always filled with light

Because the days are not always filled with light,
because the stars beam far away,
because a child cries in the night from terrors,
weeping and forgetting how to stand;

ghost of my longings,
why should there be anything other than this, my lot;

because in the hour of the lung, the blue hours breathe easy,
because the words speak as if they had a voice,
because it is their blood I know like my own;

ghost of my grandmothers, standing now before me
in human form, a young teacher in dreadlocks or with blond hair;

because there is honesty and redemption beyond office towers,
because a child welcomes me back home;

remind me of duty, remind me who it is I love.

Opportunity

She wants to go outside. You are still in your robe.
Small fingers grab the door handle and pull down,
pull out. Her bare foot steps through the small space.
You tug her inside and close the door. She gives

a shrieking cry, the one thing she worked toward
removed. *Sing the waiting song,* you implore,
but she stares longingly past the glass door
unaware and unable to understand

that you too have waited on opportunity.
She thinks only of the endless possibilities:
dirt passing through her fingers
and water pouring cold from the spigot.

Mother, Child

She is always what you make of her,
in dreams or chords of vented frustration.

She is at once an embarrassment,
joking with friends in your hometown grocery store,

and a source of pride, the lovely young woman
centered among her siblings in a family photograph.

Outside your own anger and hope,
she tends to the flowers

in her yard, pruning and transplanting,
reciting their scientific names.

You want to give her everything
and nothing.

You cannot be distant as the moon,
even though you try.

Come To Me and Drink

I know what she tastes: the ambrosia
that one morning fell in drops
from my breast to my arm. Tasting it,
my tongue recalled the white and yellow
blossoms of honeysuckle sprouting wild
along a field's edge. Collecting vine upon vine,
I'd pluck each sweet blossom, pull out
each green stamen, careful not to lose
the drop of nectar at its tip, delighting
my tongue with the watery sugar.

Now the gods put me on the vine.
The buds of my nipples are pink
and dripping. An infant plucks me dry,
a sweet smell on her breath. This liquid:
a heal-all for a stomachache, a sedative
for the sleepless child making her bed
in the field's tall grass. Her lips suckle in sleep.
Her tongue clicks in her mouth, an exercise.
The passing breeze my voice,
whispering around her ear. My arms vines
coaxing her to come to me and drink.

The Baby Discovers

Her mouth is a cavern that begins the longing
of her human life. My breast, a ball,

and the orange nose of her doll all warrant a search
by the finely tuned buds of her tongue.

Nothing escapes: bits of torn paper and a cat's whisker
are pulled from her mouth, turned over by fingers,

investigated by eyes, tried again by taste.
Her tongue will never want for these small things

so eagerly again. Once her fingertips learn
the odd tingle of sensation, once her mouth learns

certain textures it touches have no taste, no smell,
then she will yearn for the candies,

the soft creams melting in her mouth.
One day, she will seek softness and warmth

beyond my breast— the smoothness of someone else's skin
against her lips—and every inch of her body will learn

what now her tongue only knows,
what now her mouth opens itself toward.

The Dogs

Summer has arrived late
in our part of the country.
I venture outside with the dogs
where it is almost too windy

to stand, the swings moved
by the force of the breeze
rather than my daughter's legs
pumping up and back

to raise herself higher.
The dogs saunter around
the fenced-in back yard,
then circle the swing set

in a chase, growling and pulling
at collars, baring teeth.
Down the street,
neighbors bang metal and shout.

The dogs join the noise,
filling the air with warnings.
They stop and come to me
when I call their names,

happy to hear my voice
among the din, tails wagging,
wanting to know what's next,
what plans I've made.

Since I've made none,
they're happy to lean against me,
waiting for something to happen
among the trees or on the road,

looking toward me occasionally.
I can stay here all afternoon.
I am just waiting
for someone to come home.

Seduction

The infant on my lap is theirs
and he is warm and soft. He smells sweet,
like cake, a morsel of something I could eat.

I had my own baby once, but she is grown—
all knees and elbows now, gangly and gorgeous.
When I look inside my own heart,

no desire glows there. His scent wafts away.
There are oceans of want ahead, sickly sweet.
I open my sail. I have all day.

The First Step

Turning before the mirror to catch some glimmer
of who you were, you notice the hips that hang too low,

breasts enlarged with milk, nipples red and sore
from a tiny mouth's tugging.

The tear still burns where her head crowned,
a wet mess of black curls pushed out so hard

that six months later the skin still sears under healed stitches.
You wonder if your breasts want to be touched;

if your skin, when stroked, would tremble.
Why not give in, call your husband to bed?

This afternoon the child is down the hall
caught in a slumber too deep to break.

How brilliant your bodies were in that moment of conception—
how long ago, it seems.

The pieces still fit together, and here's the puzzle:
whether to let them,

whether to take that first step
toward the person you have always been.

Music for the Night, Music for the Day

To have been a farmer's bride,
rising alone, eating toast and sausage

before waking the children, husband
already out in the barn, collecting tools

for the day's work, or on a cold morning,
littering the floor with splinters of wood.

Instead, I married a poet and his child
who lie awake listening to the night,

who darken their rooms against the morning light
that I still revere no matter how I wed.

They pose questions to the dark,
follow the phases of the moon, speak to

its many eyes and mouths. From those dark
spaces they hear music, soft and indiscernible

to me, songs loosened by a beam of light
from the hall or my own voice calling out

to those chords. Lover of the morning,
I swoon to the crow's rough call and the dove's

soft whisper. They court the barred owl's
shivered chant, the dog's lonesome aria.

Each in our own worlds, I marry
the farmer and take my breakfast alone.

Julie **Brooks Barbour** received her M.F.A. in Creative Writing at UNC-Greensboro. She is a recipient of an Artist Enrichment Grant from the Kentucky Foundation for Women. Her poems have appeared in journals such as *The Greensboro Review, The Louisville Review, UCity Review, Kestrel, Waccamaw,* and *Diode,* and anthologized in *Migrations: Poetry and Prose for Life's Transitions* and *Bigger Than They Appear: Anthology of Very Short Poems.* She teaches at Lake Superior State University where she co-edits the journal *Border Crossing.*